This Journal Belongs to:

_____

ONE Question A DAY for Positivity

A Three-Year Journal

A DAILY JOURNAL FOR MANIFESTING THE LIFE YOU WANT

CASTLE POINT BOOKS

LET THE SUN SHINE IN!

Journal your way to a sunnier outlook with *One Question a Day for Positivity*, and get in the habit of sending warm, glowing, positive energy out into the world.

Whether it's writing a thank-you note, searching for a silver lining, stopping to smell the flowers, or envisioning success, there are hundreds of small but meaningful ways to radiate joy and invite new and exciting possibilities into your life.

No matter how busy you are, using a *One Question a Day* journal is a breeze. Open to the first page and read the prompt. Add the current year on the line provided and jot down a few words or sentences in response. Notice how your answers evolve year after year, and take pride in your growth.

Feel all your feelings, even the bad ones, and look back on your own wisdom when you need a lift. Manifest the good, and track your journey with *One Question a Day for Positivity*.

JANUARY 1

What went your way today?

Year: _____

_____

_____

_____

Year: _____

_____

_____

_____

Year: _____

_____

_____

_____

JANUARY 2

What positive words or vibes could you send
out into the world today?

Year: _____

_____

_____

_____

_____

Year: _____

_____

_____

_____

_____

Year: _____

_____

_____

_____

_____

JANUARY 3

Whose smile lifts your spirits?

Year: _____

_____

_____

_____

_____

Year: _____

_____

_____

_____

_____

Year: _____

_____

_____

_____

_____

JANUARY 4

What hope(s) do you have for yourself?

Year: _____

_____

_____

_____

_____

Year: _____

_____

_____

_____

_____

Year: _____

_____

_____

_____

_____

JANUARY 5

What hope(s) do you have for others?

Year: _____

_____

_____

_____

_____

Year: _____

_____

_____

_____

_____

Year: _____

_____

_____

_____

_____

JANUARY 6

What makes you a star?

Year: _____

_____

_____

_____

_____

Year: _____

_____

_____

_____

_____

Year: _____

_____

_____

_____

_____

JANUARY 7

How are you already living the
life of your dreams?

Year: _____

_____

_____

_____

_____

Year: _____

_____

_____

_____

_____

Year: _____

_____

_____

_____

_____

JANUARY 8

Whose love are you grateful to have
(or have had) in your life?

Year: _____

_____

_____

_____

_____

Year: _____

_____

_____

_____

_____

Year: _____

_____

_____

_____

_____

JANUARY 9

Draft a cheerful note to someone you
care about, then text it to them.

Year: _____

_____

_____

_____

_____

Year: _____

_____

_____

_____

_____

Year: _____

_____

_____

_____

_____

JANUARY 10

What is new and wonderful
in your life?

Year: _____

_____

_____

_____

_____

Year: _____

_____

_____

_____

_____

Year: _____

_____

_____

_____

_____

JANUARY 11

What will you accomplish in the next five years?

Year: _____

_____

_____

_____

_____

Year: _____

_____

_____

_____

_____

Year: _____

_____

_____

_____

_____

JANUARY 12

What lessons are you eager to learn?

Year: _____

_____

_____

_____

_____

Year: _____

_____

_____

_____

_____

Year: _____

_____

_____

_____

_____

JANUARY 13

What life lesson could you share
with someone else?

Year: _____

_____
_____
_____
_____

Year: _____

_____
_____
_____
_____

Year: _____

_____
_____
_____
_____

JANUARY 14

What are you free to do today?

Year: _____

_____

_____

_____

_____

Year: _____

_____

_____

_____

_____

Year: _____

_____

_____

_____

_____

JANUARY 15

What kind of partner do you deserve?

Year: _____

_____

_____

_____

_____

Year: _____

_____

_____

_____

_____

Year: _____

_____

_____

_____

_____

JANUARY 16

I am strong because _____.

Year: _____

_____

_____

_____

_____

Year: _____

_____

_____

_____

_____

Year: _____

_____

_____

_____

_____

JANUARY 17

What have you learned to love
about yourself?

Year: _____

_____

_____

_____

_____

Year: _____

_____

_____

_____

_____

Year: _____

_____

_____

_____

_____

JANUARY 18

What have you learned to love
about someone else?

Year: _____

_____

_____

_____

_____

Year: _____

_____

_____

_____

_____

Year: _____

_____

_____

_____

_____

JANUARY 19

I will be patient as I wait for _____.

Year: _____

_____

_____

_____

Year: _____

_____

_____

_____

Year: _____

_____

_____

_____

JANUARY 20

I will fight for _____.

Year: _____

_____

_____

_____

_____

Year: _____

_____

_____

_____

_____

Year: _____

_____

_____

_____

_____

JANUARY 21

What do you have under control?

Year: _____

_____

_____

_____

_____

Year: _____

_____

_____

_____

_____

Year: _____

_____

_____

_____

_____

JANUARY 22

What have you stopped trying to control?

Year: _____

_____

_____

_____

_____

Year: _____

_____

_____

_____

_____

Year: _____

_____

_____

_____

_____

JANUARY 23

Which songs do you sing in the shower?

Year: _____

_____

_____

_____

_____

Year: _____

_____

_____

_____

_____

Year: _____

_____

_____

_____

_____

JANUARY 24

What did you win at today?

Year: _____

_____

_____

_____

_____

Year: _____

_____

_____

_____

_____

Year: _____

_____

_____

_____

_____

JANUARY 25

What are you ready to try again?

Year: _____

_____

_____

_____

_____

Year: _____

_____

_____

_____

_____

Year: _____

_____

_____

_____

_____

JANUARY 26

Who sees the best in you?

Year: _____

_____

_____

_____

_____

Year: _____

_____

_____

_____

_____

Year: _____

_____

_____

_____

_____

JANUARY 27

My good habits include _____.

Year: _____

_____

_____

_____

Year: _____

_____

_____

_____

Year: _____

_____

_____

_____

JANUARY 28

I put my faith in _____.

Year: _____

_____

_____

_____

_____

Year: _____

_____

_____

_____

_____

Year: _____

_____

_____

_____

_____

JANUARY 29

When have you surpassed a goal?

Year: _____

_____

_____

_____

_____

Year: _____

_____

_____

_____

_____

Year: _____

_____

_____

_____

_____

JANUARY 30

Today I will _____.

Year: _____

_____
_____
_____
_____

Year: _____

_____
_____
_____
_____

Year: _____

_____
_____
_____
_____

JANUARY 31

Tomorrow I will _____.

Year: _____

_____
_____
_____
_____

Year: _____

_____
_____
_____
_____

Year: _____

_____
_____
_____
_____

FEBRUARY 1

I can _____ if I set my mind to it.

Year: _____

_____

_____

_____

_____

Year: _____

_____

_____

_____

_____

Year: _____

_____

_____

_____

_____

FEBRUARY 2

What are you feeling confident about today?

Year: _____

_____

_____

_____

_____

Year: _____

_____

_____

_____

_____

Year: _____

_____

_____

_____

_____

FEBRUARY 3

Which dream are you going to make happen?

Year: _____

_____

_____

_____

_____

Year: _____

_____

_____

_____

_____

Year: _____

_____

_____

_____

_____

FEBRUARY 4

What new experience awaits you?

Year: _____

_____

_____

_____

_____

Year: _____

_____

_____

_____

_____

Year: _____

_____

_____

_____

_____

FEBRUARY 5

Who inspires you?

Year: _____

_____
_____
_____
_____

Year: _____

_____
_____
_____
_____

Year: _____

_____
_____
_____
_____

FEBRUARY 6

How could you grow your finances?

Year: _____

_____
_____
_____
_____

Year: _____

_____
_____
_____
_____

Year: _____

_____
_____
_____
_____

FEBRUARY 7

How could you feed your creativity?

Year: _____

_____

_____

_____

_____

Year: _____

_____

_____

_____

_____

Year: _____

_____

_____

_____

_____

FEBRUARY 8

Which book are you looking forward to reading?

Year: _____

_____

_____

_____

_____

Year: _____

_____

_____

_____

_____

Year: _____

_____

_____

_____

_____

FEBRUARY 9

I will master the art of _____.

Year: _____

_____

_____

_____

_____

Year: _____

_____

_____

_____

_____

Year: _____

_____

_____

_____

_____

FEBRUARY 10

I'm feeling hopeful about _____.

Year: _____

_____

_____

_____

_____

Year: _____

_____

_____

_____

_____

Year: _____

_____

_____

_____

_____

FEBRUARY 11

One day I will _____.

Year: _____

_____

_____

_____

_____

Year: _____

_____

_____

_____

_____

Year: _____

_____

_____

_____

_____

FEBRUARY 12

The job of my dreams is_____.

Year: _____

_____
_____
_____
_____

Year: _____

_____
_____
_____
_____

Year: _____

_____
_____
_____
_____

FEBRUARY 13

Which past struggles give you
strength or purpose?

Year: _____

_____

_____

_____

_____

Year: _____

_____

_____

_____

_____

Year: _____

_____

_____

_____

_____

FEBRUARY 14

I will spread kindness by _____.

Year: _____

_____

_____

_____

_____

Year: _____

_____

_____

_____

_____

Year: _____

_____

_____

_____

_____

FEBRUARY 15

Never underestimate the value of _____.

Year: _____

_____
_____
_____
_____

Year: _____

_____
_____
_____
_____

Year: _____

_____
_____
_____
_____

FEBRUARY 16

What is the most beautiful thing
you can imagine?

Year: _____

_____

_____

_____

_____

Year: _____

_____

_____

_____

_____

Year: _____

_____

_____

_____

_____

FEBRUARY 17

Staying positive means _____.

Year: _____

_____

_____

_____

_____

Year: _____

_____

_____

_____

_____

Year: _____

_____

_____

_____

_____

FEBRUARY 18

When life gets hard, I can remind
myself that _____.

Year: _____

_____
_____
_____
_____

Year: _____

_____
_____
_____
_____

Year: _____

_____
_____
_____
_____

FEBRUARY 19

When have you stood up for
yourself or others?

Year: _____

_____

_____

_____

_____

Year: _____

_____

_____

_____

_____

Year: _____

_____

_____

_____

FEBRUARY 20

What compliment did you cherish?

Year: _____

_____

_____

_____

_____

Year: _____

_____

_____

_____

_____

Year: _____

_____

_____

_____

_____

FEBRUARY 21

What is something spontaneous
you could do today?

Year: _____

_____

_____

_____

_____

Year: _____

_____

_____

_____

_____

Year: _____

_____

_____

_____

_____

FEBRUARY 22

What meme makes you snort-laugh?

Year: _____

_____

_____

_____

_____

Year: _____

_____

_____

_____

_____

Year: _____

_____

_____

_____

_____

FEBRUARY 23

When has nature boosted your mood?

Year: _____

_____

_____

_____

_____

Year: _____

_____

_____

_____

_____

Year: _____

_____

_____

_____

_____

FEBRUARY 24

What gets you out of a funk?

Year: _____

_____

_____

_____

_____

Year: _____

_____

_____

_____

_____

Year: _____

_____

_____

_____

_____

FEBRUARY 25

What amazing thing can you make or do?

Year: _____

_____

_____

_____

_____

Year: _____

_____

_____

_____

_____

Year: _____

_____

_____

_____

_____

FEBRUARY 26

I feel healthiest when I _____.

Year: _____

_____

_____

_____

_____

Year: _____

_____

_____

_____

_____

Year: _____

_____

_____

_____

_____

FEBRUARY 27

One day I will travel to _____.

Year: _____

_____

_____

_____

_____

Year: _____

_____

_____

_____

_____

Year: _____

_____

_____

_____

_____

FEBRUARY 28

What worry could you turn into a wish?

Year: _____

_____

_____

_____

_____

Year: _____

_____

_____

_____

_____

Year: _____

_____

_____

_____

_____

MARCH 1

What is the best mistake you have ever made?

Year: _____

_____

_____

_____

Year: _____

_____

_____

_____

Year: _____

_____

_____

_____

MARCH 2

One benefit of getting older is _____.

Year: _____

_____

_____

_____

_____

Year: _____

_____

_____

_____

_____

Year: _____

_____

_____

_____

_____

MARCH 3

Which relationship has improved over time?

Year: _____

_____

_____

_____

_____

Year: _____

_____

_____

_____

_____

Year: _____

_____

_____

_____

_____

MARCH 4

Which moments from this year would
you be happy to relive?

Year: _____

_____

_____

_____

_____

Year: _____

_____

_____

_____

_____

Year: _____

_____

_____

_____

_____

MARCH 5

Who do you love most?

Year: _____

_____

_____

_____

_____

Year: _____

_____

_____

_____

_____

Year: _____

_____

_____

_____

_____

MARCH 6

What sparkles in your life right now?

Year: _____

_____

_____

_____

_____

Year: _____

_____

_____

_____

_____

Year: _____

_____

_____

_____

_____

MARCH 7

When are you at the top of your game?

Year: _____

_____

_____

_____

_____

Year: _____

_____

_____

_____

_____

Year: _____

_____

_____

_____

_____

MARCH 8

I am a combination of _____ and _____.

Year: _____

_____

_____

_____

_____

Year: _____

_____

_____

_____

_____

Year: _____

_____

_____

_____

_____

MARCH 9

What's your best feature?

Year: _____

_____

_____

_____

_____

Year: _____

_____

_____

_____

_____

Year: _____

_____

_____

_____

_____

MARCH 10

Who or what moves you?

Year: _____

_____

_____

_____

_____

Year: _____

_____

_____

_____

_____

Year: _____

_____

_____

_____

_____

MARCH 11

What path leads to a bright future?

Year: _____

_____

_____

_____

_____

Year: _____

_____

_____

_____

_____

Year: _____

_____

_____

_____

_____

MARCH 12

What are you no longer afraid of?

Year: _____

_____
_____
_____
_____

Year: _____

_____
_____
_____
_____

Year: _____

_____
_____
_____
_____

MARCH 13

What are you grateful for today?

Year: _____

_____

_____

_____

_____

Year: _____

_____

_____

_____

_____

Year: _____

_____

_____

_____

_____

MARCH 14

What did you recently learn about yourself?

Year: _____

_____
_____
_____
_____

Year: _____

_____
_____
_____
_____

Year: _____

_____
_____
_____
_____

MARCH 15

What's a positive way to start the day?

Year: _____

_____

_____

_____

_____

Year: _____

_____

_____

_____

_____

Year: _____

_____

_____

_____

_____

MARCH 16

What's a positive way to end the day?

Year: _____

_____

_____

_____

_____

Year: _____

_____

_____

_____

_____

Year: _____

_____

_____

_____

_____

MARCH 17

What music fills you with happiness?

Year: _____

_____

_____

_____

_____

Year: _____

_____

_____

_____

_____

Year: _____

_____

_____

_____

_____

MARCH 18

When has luck been on your side?

Year: _____

_____
_____
_____
_____

Year: _____

_____
_____
_____
_____

Year: _____

_____
_____
_____
_____

MARCH 19

What have you moved on from?

Year: _____

_____
_____
_____
_____

Year: _____

_____
_____
_____
_____

Year: _____

_____
_____
_____
_____

MARCH 20

Which season suits your personality
best? Explain.

Year: _____

_____

_____

_____

_____

Year: _____

_____

_____

_____

_____

Year: _____

_____

_____

_____

_____

MARCH 21

What were you happy to discover?

Year: _____

_____
_____
_____
_____

Year: _____

_____
_____
_____
_____

Year: _____

_____
_____
_____
_____

MARCH 22

What's the best way to share your joy?

Year: _____

_____
_____
_____
_____

Year: _____

_____
_____
_____
_____

Year: _____

_____
_____
_____
_____

MARCH 23

How can someone tell when you're
in a good mood?

Year: _____

_____

_____

_____

_____

Year: _____

_____

_____

_____

_____

Year: _____

_____

_____

_____

_____

MARCH 24

How well did you treat yourself today?

Year: _____

_____

_____

_____

_____

Year: _____

_____

_____

_____

_____

Year: _____

_____

_____

_____

_____

MARCH 25

What would you title this chapter of your life?

Year: _____

_____

_____

_____

_____

Year: _____

_____

_____

_____

_____

Year: _____

_____

_____

_____

_____

MARCH 26

What three wishes would you like
to make today?

Year: _____

_____

_____

_____

_____

Year: _____

_____

_____

_____

_____

Year: _____

_____

_____

_____

_____

MARCH 27

Who is the sun in your sky?

Year: _____

_____

_____

_____

_____

Year: _____

_____

_____

_____

_____

Year: _____

_____

_____

_____

_____

MARCH 28

When have you been rewarded for
your hard work?

Year: _____

_____
_____
_____
_____

Year: _____

_____
_____
_____
_____

Year: _____

_____
_____
_____
_____

MARCH 29

What adventure are you ready
to embark on?

Year: _____

_____

_____

_____

_____

Year: _____

_____

_____

_____

_____

Year: _____

_____

_____

_____

_____

MARCH 30

What makes you proud?

Year: _____

_____

_____

_____

_____

Year: _____

_____

_____

_____

_____

Year: _____

_____

_____

_____

_____

MARCH 31

What gifts are in store for you today?

Year: _____

_____

_____

_____

_____

Year: _____

_____

_____

_____

_____

Year: _____

_____

_____

_____

_____

APRIL 1

What is your "wow" factor?

Year: _____

_____

_____

_____

_____

Year: _____

_____

_____

_____

_____

Year: _____

_____

_____

_____

_____

APRIL 2

Who energizes you?

Year: _____

_____

_____

_____

_____

Year: _____

_____

_____

_____

_____

Year: _____

_____

_____

_____

_____

APRIL 3

What helps you find calm?

Year: _____

_____

_____

_____

_____

Year: _____

_____

_____

_____

_____

Year: _____

_____

_____

_____

_____

APRIL 4

Life is _____.

Year: _____

_____

_____

_____

_____

Year: _____

_____

_____

_____

_____

Year: _____

_____

_____

_____

_____

APRIL 5

What is the best thing that
happened today?

Year: _____

_____
_____
_____
_____

Year: _____

_____
_____
_____
_____

Year: _____

_____
_____
_____
_____

APRIL 6

Rewrite a negative thought as
a positive one.

Year: _____

_____

_____

_____

_____

Year: _____

_____

_____

_____

_____

Year: _____

_____

_____

_____

_____

APRIL 7

Where do you see potential?

Year: _____

_____

_____

_____

_____

Year: _____

_____

_____

_____

_____

Year: _____

_____

_____

_____

_____

APRIL 8

What is the best part of your job?

Year: _____

_____

_____

_____

_____

Year: _____

_____

_____

_____

_____

Year: _____

_____

_____

_____

_____

APRIL 9

Which poem lifts your spirits?

Year: _____

_____

_____

_____

_____

Year: _____

_____

_____

_____

_____

Year: _____

_____

_____

_____

_____

APRIL 10

Which colors make your heart happy?

Year: _____

_____
_____
_____
_____

Year: _____

_____
_____
_____
_____

Year: _____

_____
_____
_____
_____

APRIL 11

Which friendship are you grateful for?

Year: _____

_____
_____
_____
_____

Year: _____

_____
_____
_____
_____

Year: _____

_____
_____
_____
_____

APRIL 12

What could you win an award for some day?

Year: _____

_____

_____

_____

_____

Year: _____

_____

_____

_____

_____

Year: _____

_____

_____

_____

_____

APRIL 13

What was the first happy thought that
came to mind today?

Year: _____

_____
_____
_____
_____

Year: _____

_____
_____
_____
_____

Year: _____

_____
_____
_____
_____

APRIL 14

What's your earliest happy memory?

Year: _____

_____

_____

_____

_____

Year: _____

_____

_____

_____

_____

Year: _____

_____

_____

_____

_____

APRIL 15

What makes your life full?

Year: _____

_____

_____

_____

_____

Year: _____

_____

_____

_____

_____

Year: _____

_____

_____

_____

_____

APRIL 16

Which pastime do you enjoy most?

Year: _____

_____

_____

_____

_____

Year: _____

_____

_____

_____

_____

Year: _____

_____

_____

_____

_____

APRIL 17

Which memory makes you laugh?

Year: _____

_____

_____

_____

_____

Year: _____

_____

_____

_____

_____

Year: _____

_____

_____

_____

_____

APRIL 18

What do you love most about your life?

Year: _____

_____

_____

_____

_____

Year: _____

_____

_____

_____

_____

Year: _____

_____

_____

_____

_____

APRIL 19

What do you like about where you live?

Year: _____

_____

_____

_____

_____

Year: _____

_____

_____

_____

_____

Year: _____

_____

_____

_____

_____

APRIL 20

What do you know to be true?

Year: _____

_____

_____

_____

_____

Year: _____

_____

_____

_____

_____

Year: _____

_____

_____

_____

_____

APRIL 21

What have you achieved this week?

Year: _____

_____
_____
_____
_____

Year: _____

_____
_____
_____
_____

Year: _____

_____
_____
_____
_____

APRIL 22

Who would you like to meet?

Year: _____

_____

_____

_____

_____

Year: _____

_____

_____

_____

_____

Year: _____

_____

_____

_____

_____

APRIL 23

What is the icing on the
cake of today?

Year: _____

_____

_____

_____

_____

Year: _____

_____

_____

_____

_____

Year: _____

_____

_____

_____

_____

APRIL 24

How do you want to celebrate
your next birthday?

Year: _____

_____

_____

_____

_____

Year: _____

_____

_____

_____

_____

Year: _____

_____

_____

_____

_____

APRIL 25

When was the last time you danced
your heart out?

Year: _____

_____

_____

_____

_____

Year: _____

_____

_____

_____

_____

Year: _____

_____

_____

_____

_____

APRIL 26

Which foods do you enjoy wholeheartedly?

Year: _____

_____

_____

_____

_____

Year: _____

_____

_____

_____

_____

Year: _____

_____

_____

_____

APRIL 27

What do you cherish most in life?

Year: _____

_____

_____

_____

_____

Year: _____

_____

_____

_____

_____

Year: _____

_____

_____

_____

_____

APRIL 28

What's the best thing about your family?

Year: _____

_____
_____
_____
_____

Year: _____

_____
_____
_____
_____

Year: _____

_____
_____
_____
_____

APRIL 29

What vacation would you
love to take?

Year: _____

_____

_____

_____

_____

Year: _____

_____

_____

_____

_____

Year: _____

_____

_____

_____

_____

APRIL 30

What is one stressor you could
remove from your life?

Year: _____

_____
_____
_____
_____

Year: _____

_____
_____
_____
_____

Year: _____

_____
_____
_____
_____

MAY 1

Where is your happy place?

Year: _____

_____

_____

_____

Year: _____

_____

_____

_____

Year: _____

_____

_____

_____

MAY 2

How can you spread positivity today?

Year: _____

_____

_____

_____

_____

Year: _____

_____

_____

_____

_____

Year: _____

_____

_____

_____

_____

MAY 3

Who are the most positive
people you know?

Year: _____

_____

_____

_____

_____

Year: _____

_____

_____

_____

_____

Year: _____

_____

_____

_____

_____

MAY 4

What makes you feel good
about the future?

Year: _____

_____

_____

_____

_____

Year: _____

_____

_____

_____

_____

Year: _____

_____

_____

_____

_____

MAY 5

Who do you want to become?

Year: _____

_____

_____

_____

_____

Year: _____

_____

_____

_____

_____

Year: _____

_____

_____

_____

_____

MAY 6

What warms your heart?

Year: _____

_____

_____

_____

_____

Year: _____

_____

_____

_____

_____

Year: _____

_____

_____

_____

_____

MAY 7

What quote lifts your spirits?

Year: _____

_____

_____

_____

_____

Year: _____

_____

_____

_____

_____

Year: _____

_____

_____

_____

_____

MAY 8

Who looks to you for guidance or advice?

Year: _____

_____

_____

_____

_____

Year: _____

_____

_____

_____

_____

Year: _____

_____

_____

_____

_____

MAY 9

What fun plans could you make today?

Year: _____

_____

_____

_____

_____

Year: _____

_____

_____

_____

_____

Year: _____

_____

_____

_____

_____

MAY 10

What new and joyful tradition could
you start today?

Year: _____

_____

_____

_____

_____

Year: _____

_____

_____

_____

_____

Year: _____

_____

_____

_____

_____

MAY 11

What good habit could you add to
your daily routine?

Year: _____

_____
_____
_____
_____

Year: _____

_____
_____
_____
_____

Year: _____

_____
_____
_____
_____

MAY 12

What positive experience
did you have today?

Year: _____

_____

_____

_____

_____

Year: _____

_____

_____

_____

_____

Year: _____

_____

_____

_____

_____

MAY 13

Today I'll look for the good in _____.

Year: _____

_____

_____

_____

_____

Year: _____

_____

_____

_____

_____

Year: _____

_____

_____

_____

_____

MAY 14

What small luxury makes the
biggest difference?

Year: _____

_____

_____

_____

_____

Year: _____

_____

_____

_____

_____

Year: _____

_____

_____

_____

_____

MAY 15

I will add more _____ to my life.

Year: _____

_____

_____

_____

_____

Year: _____

_____

_____

_____

_____

Year: _____

_____

_____

_____

_____

MAY 16

Who or what deserves your 5-star rating?

Year: _____

_____

_____

_____

_____

Year: _____

_____

_____

_____

_____

Year: _____

_____

_____

_____

_____

MAY 17

Today I will accomplish _____.

Year: _____

_____
_____
_____
_____

Year: _____

_____
_____
_____
_____

Year: _____

_____
_____
_____
_____

MAY 18

Stop to admire the view today—any view.
Describe it below.

Year: _____

_____

_____

_____

_____

Year: _____

_____

_____

_____

Year: _____

_____

_____

_____

_____

MAY 19

Maybe I can't win 'em all, but I can _____.

Year: _____

_____

_____

_____

_____

Year: _____

_____

_____

_____

_____

Year: _____

_____

_____

_____

_____

MAY 20

What are you looking forward to this weekend?

Year: _____

_____

_____

_____

_____

Year: _____

_____

_____

_____

_____

Year: _____

_____

_____

_____

_____

MAY 21

Find a positive article in today's news.
Write the headline below.

Year: _____

_____

_____

_____

_____

Year: _____

_____

_____

_____

_____

Year: _____

_____

_____

_____

_____

MAY 22

Make a positive prediction
about this year.

Year: _____

_____

_____

_____

_____

Year: _____

_____

_____

_____

_____

Year: _____

_____

_____

_____

_____

MAY 23

What fills you with promise?

Year: _____

_____

_____

_____

_____

Year: _____

_____

_____

_____

_____

Year: _____

_____

_____

_____

_____

MAY 24

Who are you looking forward to seeing?

Year: _____

_____

_____

_____

_____

Year: _____

_____

_____

_____

_____

Year: _____

_____

_____

_____

_____

MAY 25

What will your generation accomplish?

Year: _____

_____

_____

_____

_____

Year: _____

_____

_____

_____

_____

Year: _____

_____

_____

_____

_____

MAY 26

What future event are you
excited about attending?

Year: _____

_____

_____

_____

_____

Year: _____

_____

_____

_____

_____

Year: _____

_____

_____

_____

_____

MAY 27

When have you discovered a silver lining?

Year: _____

_____

_____

_____

_____

Year: _____

_____

_____

_____

_____

Year: _____

_____

_____

_____

_____

MAY 28

What made you smile today?

Year: _____

_____

_____

_____

_____

Year: _____

_____

_____

_____

Year: _____

_____

_____

_____

MAY 29

Who did you make smile today?

Year: _____

_____
_____
_____
_____

Year: _____

_____
_____
_____
_____

Year: _____

_____
_____
_____
_____

MAY 30

What lasts forever?

Year: _____

_____

_____

_____

_____

Year: _____

_____

_____

_____

_____

Year: _____

_____

_____

_____

_____

MAY 31

What is the most promising thing
you've heard in a while?

Year: _____

_____

_____

_____

_____

Year: _____

_____

_____

_____

_____

Year: _____

_____

_____

_____

_____

JUNE 1

Who or what intrigues you?

Year: _____

_____

_____

_____

_____

Year: _____

_____

_____

_____

_____

Year: _____

_____

_____

_____

_____

JUNE 2

How can you invest in your
future or yourself?

Year: _____

_____

_____

_____

_____

Year: _____

_____

_____

_____

_____

Year: _____

_____

_____

_____

_____

JUNE 3

What is the best thing about
being your age?

Year: _____

_____

_____

_____

_____

Year: _____

_____

_____

_____

_____

Year: _____

_____

_____

_____

_____

JUNE 4

What do you love most about your home?

Year: _____

_____

_____

_____

_____

Year: _____

_____

_____

_____

_____

Year: _____

_____

_____

_____

_____

JUNE 5

What wisdom are you eager to share?

Year: _____

_____

_____

_____

_____

Year: _____

_____

_____

_____

Year: _____

_____

_____

_____

JUNE 6

What always makes you laugh?

Year: _____

_____

_____

_____

_____

Year: _____

_____

_____

_____

_____

Year: _____

_____

_____

_____

_____

JUNE 7

What makes you beautiful?

Year: _____

_____

_____

_____

_____

Year: _____

_____

_____

_____

_____

Year: _____

_____

_____

_____

_____

JUNE 8

What makes you fierce?

Year: _____

_____

_____

_____

_____

Year: _____

_____

_____

_____

_____

Year: _____

_____

_____

_____

_____

JUNE 9

In what simple pleasure do you indulge?

Year: _____

_____

_____

_____

_____

Year: _____

_____

_____

_____

_____

Year: _____

_____

_____

_____

_____

JUNE 10

Write a positive affirmation for yourself.

Year: _____

_____

_____

_____

_____

Year: _____

_____

_____

_____

_____

Year: _____

_____

_____

_____

_____

JUNE 11

My strength comes from _____.

Year: _____

_____

_____

_____

_____

Year: _____

_____

_____

_____

_____

Year: _____

_____

_____

_____

_____

JUNE 12

When have you adapted well to change?

Year: _____

_____

_____

_____

_____

Year: _____

_____

_____

_____

_____

Year: _____

_____

_____

_____

_____

JUNE 13

What ideas are you eager to share?

Year: _____

_____

_____

_____

_____

Year: _____

_____

_____

_____

Year: _____

_____

_____

_____

JUNE 14

Today I will remind myself that _____.

Year: _____

_____

_____

_____

_____

Year: _____

_____

_____

_____

_____

Year: _____

_____

_____

_____

_____

JUNE 15

There's no time like the present to _____.

Year: _____
_____
_____
_____
_____

Year: _____
_____
_____
_____
_____

Year: _____
_____
_____
_____
_____

JUNE 16

What are you grateful for today?

Year: _____

_____

_____

_____

_____

Year: _____

_____

_____

_____

_____

Year: _____

_____

_____

_____

_____

JUNE 17

What are you destined for?

Year: _____

_____

_____

_____

_____

Year: _____

_____

_____

_____

_____

Year: _____

_____

_____

_____

_____

JUNE 18

What did you stop to appreciate today?

Year: _____

_____
_____
_____
_____

Year: _____

_____
_____
_____
_____

Year: _____

_____
_____
_____
_____

JUNE 19

What are you most looking forward
to this week?

Year: _____

_____

_____

_____

_____

Year: _____

_____

_____

_____

_____

Year: _____

_____

_____

_____

_____

JUNE 20

What dream has come
true for you?

Year: _____

_____

_____

_____

_____

Year: _____

_____

_____

_____

_____

Year: _____

_____

_____

_____

_____

JUNE 21

What positive change are you
excited about making?

Year: _____

_____

_____

_____

_____

Year: _____

_____

_____

_____

_____

Year: _____

_____

_____

_____

_____

JUNE 22

What do you want to happen today?

Year: _____

_____

_____

_____

_____

Year: _____

_____

_____

_____

_____

Year: _____

_____

_____

_____

_____

JUNE 23

What is worth the risk?

Year: _____

_____
_____
_____
_____

Year: _____

_____
_____
_____
_____

Year: _____

_____
_____
_____
_____

JUNE 24

How have you grown as a person?

Year: _____

_____

_____

_____

_____

Year: _____

_____

_____

_____

_____

Year: _____

_____

_____

_____

_____

JUNE 25

What are you the king or queen of?

Year: _____

_____
_____
_____
_____

Year: _____

_____
_____
_____
_____

Year: _____

_____
_____
_____
_____

JUNE 26

What's the best part about being you?

Year: _____

_____

_____

_____

_____

Year: _____

_____

_____

_____

_____

Year: _____

_____

_____

_____

_____

JUNE 27

The world is my _____.

Year: _____

_____
_____
_____
_____

Year: _____

_____
_____
_____
_____

Year: _____

_____
_____
_____
_____

JUNE 28

I will never give up on _____.

Year: _____

_____

_____

_____

_____

Year: _____

_____

_____

_____

_____

Year: _____

_____

_____

_____

_____

JUNE 29

What movie has the happiest ending?

Year: _____

_____

_____

_____

_____

Year: _____

_____

_____

_____

_____

Year: _____

_____

_____

_____

_____

JUNE 30

Who would you cast in the movie
version of your life?

Year: _____

_____

_____

_____

_____

Year: _____

_____

_____

_____

_____

Year: _____

_____

_____

_____

_____

JULY *1*

What does your heart want today?

Year: _____

_____

_____

_____

_____

Year: _____

_____

_____

_____

_____

Year: _____

_____

_____

_____

JULY 2

What is only just beginning?

Year: _____

_____

_____

_____

_____

Year: _____

_____

_____

_____

_____

Year: _____

_____

_____

_____

_____

JULY 3

_____ is food for the soul.

Year: _____

_____

_____

_____

_____

Year: _____

_____

_____

_____

_____

Year: _____

_____

_____

_____

_____

JULY 4

List three compliments for yourself.

Year: _____

_____

_____

_____

_____

Year: _____

_____

_____

_____

_____

Year: _____

_____

_____

_____

_____

JULY 5

Who encourages you to go for it?

Year: _____

_____
_____
_____
_____

Year: _____

_____
_____
_____
_____

Year: _____

_____
_____
_____
_____

JULY 6

What is your greatest source of comfort?

Year: _____

_____

_____

_____

_____

Year: _____

_____

_____

_____

_____

Year: _____

_____

_____

_____

_____

JULY 7

Describe how it feels to be happy.

Year: _____

_____

_____

_____

_____

Year: _____

_____

_____

_____

_____

Year: _____

_____

_____

_____

_____

JULY 8

What could you yell from the rooftops today?

Year: _____

_____
_____
_____
_____

Year: _____

_____
_____
_____
_____

Year: _____

_____
_____
_____
_____

JULY 9

What do you want to learn more about?

Year: _____

_____
_____
_____
_____

Year: _____

_____
_____
_____
_____

Year: _____

_____
_____
_____
_____

JULY 10

What makes you fortunate?

Year: _____

_____

_____

_____

_____

Year: _____

_____

_____

_____

_____

Year: _____

_____

_____

_____

_____

JULY 11

What mountain has turned
into a molehill?

Year: _____

_____

_____

_____

_____

Year: _____

_____

_____

_____

_____

Year: _____

_____

_____

_____

_____

JULY 12

How does positivity affect your relationships?

Year: _____

_____

_____

_____

_____

Year: _____

_____

_____

_____

_____

Year: _____

_____

_____

_____

_____

JULY 13

When has negativity gotten in your way?

Year: _____

_____

_____

_____

_____

Year: _____

_____

_____

_____

_____

Year: _____

_____

_____

_____

_____

JULY 14

What makes you want to rise and shine?

Year: _____

_____

_____

_____

_____

Year: _____

_____

_____

_____

_____

Year: _____

_____

_____

_____

_____

JULY 15

Why should you be proud of yourself today?

Year: _____

_____

_____

_____

_____

Year: _____

_____

_____

_____

_____

Year: _____

_____

_____

_____

_____

JULY 16

Who can you reach out to in times of struggle?

Year: _____

_____

_____

_____

Year: _____

_____

_____

_____

Year: _____

_____

_____

_____

JULY 17

Who did you connect with today?

Year: _____

_____

_____

_____

_____

Year: _____

_____

_____

_____

_____

Year: _____

_____

_____

_____

_____

JULY 18

One fantasy I'd like to live out is _____.

Year: _____

_____

_____

_____

_____

Year: _____

_____

_____

_____

_____

Year: _____

_____

_____

_____

_____

JULY 19

What are you interested in trying?

Year: _____

_____

_____

_____

_____

Year: _____

_____

_____

_____

_____

Year: _____

_____

_____

_____

_____

JULY 20

Describe the perfect day.

Year: _____

_____

_____

_____

_____

Year: _____

_____

_____

_____

_____

Year: _____

_____

_____

_____

_____

JULY 21

What felt good today?

Year: _____

_____
_____
_____
_____

Year: _____

_____
_____
_____
_____

Year: _____

_____
_____
_____
_____

JULY 22

What gives you a brighter outlook?

Year: _____

_____

_____

_____

_____

Year: _____

_____

_____

_____

_____

Year: _____

_____

_____

_____

_____

JULY 23

What's the best way to fall asleep?

Year: _____

_____
_____
_____
_____

Year: _____

_____
_____
_____
_____

Year: _____

_____
_____
_____
_____

JULY 24

I am determined to _____.

Year: _____

_____

_____

_____

_____

Year: _____

_____

_____

_____

_____

Year: _____

_____

_____

_____

_____

JULY 25

Who underestimates you?

Year: _____

_____

_____

_____

_____

Year: _____

_____

_____

_____

_____

Year: _____

_____

_____

_____

_____

JULY 26

What will you take a moment to
celebrate today?

Year: _____

_____

_____

_____

_____

Year: _____

_____

_____

_____

_____

Year: _____

_____

_____

_____

_____

JULY 27

What are you ready to change?

Year: _____

_____

_____

_____

_____

Year: _____

_____

_____

_____

_____

Year: _____

_____

_____

_____

_____

JULY 28

What are your superpowers?

Year: _____

_____

_____

_____

_____

Year: _____

_____

_____

_____

_____

Year: _____

_____

_____

_____

_____

JULY 29

How are your weaknesses also your strengths?

Year: _____

_____

_____

_____

_____

Year: _____

_____

_____

_____

_____

Year: _____

_____

_____

_____

_____

JULY 30

What side of you do you keep hidden?
How can you coax it out?

Year: _____

_____

_____

_____

_____

Year: _____

_____

_____

_____

_____

Year: _____

_____

_____

_____

_____

JULY 31

What motivates you?

Year: _____

_____
_____
_____
_____

Year: _____

_____
_____
_____
_____

Year: _____

_____
_____
_____

AUGUST 1

How will you embrace this day?

Year: _____

_____

_____

_____

_____

Year: _____

_____

_____

_____

_____

Year: _____

_____

_____

_____

_____

AUGUST 2

What are you thankful to have in your life?

Year: _____

_____

_____

_____

_____

Year: _____

_____

_____

_____

_____

Year: _____

_____

_____

_____

_____

AUGUST 3

What is today's motto?

Year: _____

_____

_____

_____

_____

Year: _____

_____

_____

_____

_____

Year: _____

_____

_____

_____

_____

AUGUST 4

Who is your biggest cheerleader?

Year: _____

_____

_____

_____

_____

Year: _____

_____

_____

_____

_____

Year: _____

_____

_____

_____

_____

AUGUST 5

What does it mean to *live large*?

Year: _____

_____

_____

_____

Year: _____

_____

_____

_____

Year: _____

_____

_____

_____

AUGUST 6

What's getting easier?

Year: _____

_____

_____

_____

_____

Year: _____

_____

_____

_____

_____

Year: _____

_____

_____

_____

_____

AUGUST 7

What's never been better?

Year: _____

_____
_____
_____
_____

Year: _____

_____
_____
_____
_____

Year: _____

_____
_____
_____
_____

AUGUST 8

I can always rely on _____.

Year: _____
_____
_____
_____
_____

Year: _____
_____
_____
_____
_____

Year: _____
_____
_____
_____
_____

AUGUST 9

The road to happiness is paved
with _____.

Year: _____

_____

_____

_____

_____

Year: _____

_____

_____

_____

_____

Year: _____

_____

_____

_____

_____

AUGUST 10

What will you accomplish
this year?

Year: _____

_____

_____

_____

_____

Year: _____

_____

_____

_____

_____

Year: _____

_____

_____

_____

_____

AUGUST 11

To what would you give a 5-star review?

Year: _____

_____

_____

_____

Year: _____

_____

_____

_____

Year: _____

_____

_____

_____

AUGUST 12

What part of your life is ready for a makeover?

Year: _____

_____

_____

_____

_____

Year: _____

_____

_____

_____

_____

Year: _____

_____

_____

_____

_____

AUGUST 13

Look for beauty in nature today.
What do you see?

Year: _____

_____

_____

_____

_____

Year: _____

_____

_____

_____

_____

Year: _____

_____

_____

_____

_____

AUGUST 14

Who looks up to you?

Year: _____

_____
_____
_____
_____

Year: _____

_____
_____
_____
_____

Year: _____

_____
_____
_____
_____

AUGUST 15

What is the best thing about being single?

Year: _____

_____

_____

_____

_____

Year: _____

_____

_____

_____

_____

Year: _____

_____

_____

_____

_____

AUGUST 16

What is the best thing about being
in a relationship?

Year: _____

_____

_____

_____

_____

Year: _____

_____

_____

_____

_____

Year: _____

_____

_____

_____

_____

AUGUST 17

I'm a fantastic _____.

Year: _____

_____

_____

_____

_____

Year: _____

_____

_____

_____

_____

Year: _____

_____

_____

_____

_____

AUGUST 18

This is the perfect weather
for _____.

Year: _____

_____

_____

_____

_____

Year: _____

_____

_____

_____

_____

Year: _____

_____

_____

_____

_____

AUGUST 19

What comes easily to you?

Year: _____

_____

_____

_____

_____

Year: _____

_____

_____

_____

_____

Year: _____

_____

_____

_____

_____

AUGUST 20

Who is your copilot?

Year: _____

_____

_____

_____

_____

Year: _____

_____

_____

_____

_____

Year: _____

_____

_____

_____

_____

AUGUST 21

What feels just right today?

Year: _____

_____

_____

_____

_____

Year: _____

_____

_____

_____

_____

Year: _____

_____

_____

_____

_____

AUGUST 22

What can you visualize when you
need a mood lift?

Year: _____

_____

_____

_____

_____

Year: _____

_____

_____

_____

_____

Year: _____

_____

_____

_____

AUGUST 23

What word is impossible to say
without smiling?

Year: _____

_____

_____

_____

_____

Year: _____

_____

_____

_____

_____

Year: _____

_____

_____

_____

_____

AUGUST 24

Who needs a hug from you today?

Year: _____

_____

_____

_____

_____

Year: _____

_____

_____

_____

_____

Year: _____

_____

_____

_____

_____

AUGUST 25

I have the courage to _____.

Year: _____

_____

_____

_____

_____

Year: _____

_____

_____

_____

_____

Year: _____

_____

_____

_____

_____

AUGUST 26

I'm at peace with _____.

Year: _____

_____

_____

_____

_____

Year: _____

_____

_____

_____

_____

Year: _____

_____

_____

_____

_____

AUGUST 27

A small win for today was _____.

Year: _____

_____

_____

_____

_____

Year: _____

_____

_____

_____

_____

Year: _____

_____

_____

_____

_____

AUGUST 28

What are you open-minded about?

Year: _____

_____

_____

_____

_____

Year: _____

_____

_____

_____

_____

Year: _____

_____

_____

_____

_____

AUGUST 29

How could you make a difference
in someone's life?

Year: _____

_____

_____

_____

_____

Year: _____

_____

_____

_____

_____

Year: _____

_____

_____

_____

_____

AUGUST 30

What is the best way to turn a bad
day into a good one?

Year: _____

_____

_____

_____

_____

Year: _____

_____

_____

_____

_____

Year: _____

_____

_____

_____

_____

AUGUST 31

Which emoji captures your vibe today?
Draw it or describe it.

Year: _____

_____

_____

_____

_____

Year: _____

_____

_____

_____

_____

Year: _____

_____

_____

_____

_____

SEPTEMBER 1

Write down a good joke, then tell it to
someone who will appreciate it.

Year: _____

_____

_____

_____

_____

Year: _____

_____

_____

_____

_____

Year: _____

_____

_____

_____

_____

SEPTEMBER 2

What surprise would make your day?

Year: _____

_____

_____

_____

_____

Year: _____

_____

_____

_____

_____

Year: _____

_____

_____

_____

_____

SEPTEMBER 3

Who are you happy to know?

Year: _____

_____

_____

_____

_____

Year: _____

_____

_____

_____

_____

Year: _____

_____

_____

_____

_____

SEPTEMBER 4

What's the best way to handle
negativity from others?

Year: _____

_____

_____

_____

_____

Year: _____

_____

_____

_____

_____

Year: _____

_____

_____

_____

_____

SEPTEMBER 5

Hum the first happy song that comes to mind.
Jot down the best lyrics.

Year: _____

_____

_____

_____

_____

Year: _____

_____

_____

_____

_____

Year: _____

_____

_____

_____

_____

SEPTEMBER 6

How are you your own best guide?

Year: _____

_____

_____

_____

_____

Year: _____

_____

_____

_____

_____

Year: _____

_____

_____

_____

_____

SEPTEMBER 7

Where do you want to go this year?

Year: _____

_____

_____

_____

_____

Year: _____

_____

_____

_____

_____

Year: _____

_____

_____

_____

_____

SEPTEMBER 8

How far have you come?

Year: _____

_____

_____

_____

_____

Year: _____

_____

_____

_____

_____

Year: _____

_____

_____

_____

_____

SEPTEMBER 9

Whose art inspires you?

Year: _____

_____

_____

_____

_____

Year: _____

_____

_____

_____

_____

Year: _____

_____

_____

_____

_____

SEPTEMBER 10

Which charity is making the world a better place? How could you help?

Year: _____

_____

_____

_____

_____

Year: _____

_____

_____

_____

_____

Year: _____

_____

_____

_____

_____

SEPTEMBER 11

What will you remember most
about this day?

Year: _____

_____

_____

_____

_____

Year: _____

_____

_____

_____

_____

Year: _____

_____

_____

_____

_____

SEPTEMBER 12

What don't you need as much as
you thought you did?

Year: _____

_____

_____

_____

_____

Year: _____

_____

_____

_____

_____

Year: _____

_____

_____

_____

_____

SEPTEMBER 13

What was the best thing your
parent(s) taught you?

Year: _____

_____

_____

_____

_____

Year: _____

_____

_____

_____

_____

Year: _____

_____

_____

_____

_____

SEPTEMBER 14

Who do you think of as a role model?

Year: _____

_____

_____

_____

_____

Year: _____

_____

_____

_____

_____

Year: _____

_____

_____

_____

_____

SEPTEMBER 15

What's gleaming on the horizon today?

Year: _____

_____
_____
_____
_____

Year: _____

_____
_____
_____
_____

Year: _____

_____
_____
_____
_____

SEPTEMBER 16

How can you turn a foe into a friend?

Year: _____

_____

_____

_____

_____

Year: _____

_____

_____

_____

_____

Year: _____

_____

_____

_____

_____

SEPTEMBER 17

Describe yourself in a purely positive light.

Year: _____

_____

_____

_____

_____

Year: _____

_____

_____

_____

_____

Year: _____

_____

_____

_____

_____

SEPTEMBER 18

What kind words do you have
for yourself today?

Year: _____

_____

_____

_____

_____

Year: _____

_____

_____

_____

_____

Year: _____

_____

_____

_____

_____

SEPTEMBER 19

Today is a good day to _____.

Year: _____

_____

_____

_____

_____

Year: _____

_____

_____

_____

_____

Year: _____

_____

_____

_____

_____

SEPTEMBER 20

What do you prefer to do alone?

Year: _____

_____

_____

_____

_____

Year: _____

_____

_____

_____

_____

Year: _____

_____

_____

_____

_____

SEPTEMBER 21

Who's always on your side?

Year: _____

_____
_____
_____
_____

Year: _____

_____
_____
_____
_____

Year: _____

_____
_____
_____
_____

SEPTEMBER 22

What makes you an excellent friend?

Year: _____

_____

_____

_____

_____

Year: _____

_____

_____

_____

_____

Year: _____

_____

_____

_____

_____

SEPTEMBER 23

What makes you a good sister, brother,
son, or daughter?

Year: _____

_____

_____

_____

_____

Year: _____

_____

_____

_____

_____

Year: _____

_____

_____

_____

_____

SEPTEMBER 24

List three things you're happy about today.

Year: _____

_____

_____

_____

_____

Year: _____

_____

_____

_____

_____

Year: _____

_____

_____

_____

_____

SEPTEMBER 25

Feel all your feelings today, and identify
some of them below.

Year: _____

_____

_____

_____

_____

Year: _____

_____

_____

_____

_____

Year: _____

_____

_____

_____

_____

SEPTEMBER 26

How could you end this day on a high note?

Year: _____

_____

_____

_____

_____

Year: _____

_____

_____

_____

_____

Year: _____

_____

_____

_____

_____

SEPTEMBER 27

What matters most?

Year: _____

_____

_____

_____

_____

Year: _____

_____

_____

_____

_____

Year: _____

_____

_____

_____

_____

SEPTEMBER 28

When have you felt free to make mistakes?

Year: _____

_____

_____

_____

_____

Year: _____

_____

_____

_____

_____

Year: _____

_____

_____

_____

_____

SEPTEMBER 29

What subjects do you know a lot about?

Year: _____

_____

_____

_____

_____

Year: _____

_____

_____

_____

_____

Year: _____

_____

_____

_____

_____

SEPTEMBER 30

What has the biggest influence
on your mood?

Year: _____

_____

_____

_____

_____

Year: _____

_____

_____

_____

_____

Year: _____

_____

_____

_____

_____

OCTOBER 1

What is the best way to handle
criticism from others?

Year: _____

_____

_____

_____

_____

Year: _____

_____

_____

_____

_____

Year: _____

_____

_____

_____

_____

OCTOBER 2

Which path are you glad you chose?

Year: _____

_____

_____

_____

_____

Year: _____

_____

_____

_____

_____

Year: _____

_____

_____

_____

_____

OCTOBER 3

Which celebrity would you love to meet?

Year: _____

_____

_____

_____

_____

Year: _____

_____

_____

_____

_____

Year: _____

_____

_____

_____

_____

OCTOBER 4

When have you felt a sense of purpose?

Year: _____

_____

_____

_____

_____

Year: _____

_____

_____

_____

_____

Year: _____

_____

_____

_____

_____

OCTOBER 5

When have you benefited from
following your instincts?

Year: _____

_____

_____

_____

_____

Year: _____

_____

_____

_____

_____

Year: _____

_____

_____

_____

_____

OCTOBER 6

Who do you know you can trust?

Year: _____

_____

_____

_____

_____

Year: _____

_____

_____

_____

_____

Year: _____

_____

_____

_____

_____

OCTOBER 7

What sound calms you or brings back
good memories?

Year: _____

_____

_____

_____

_____

Year: _____

_____

_____

_____

_____

Year: _____

_____

_____

_____

_____

OCTOBER 8

What did you work hard to do today?

Year: _____

_____
_____
_____
_____

Year: _____

_____
_____
_____
_____

Year: _____

_____
_____
_____
_____

OCTOBER 9

_____ makes my life complete.

Year: _____

_____

_____

_____

_____

Year: _____

_____

_____

_____

_____

Year: _____

_____

_____

_____

_____

OCTOBER 10

What makes a day go from blah to hoorah?

Year: _____

_____

_____

_____

Year: _____

_____

_____

_____

Year: _____

_____

_____

_____

OCTOBER 11

When have you benefited from the
kindness of strangers?

Year: _____

_____

_____

_____

_____

Year: _____

_____

_____

_____

_____

Year: _____

_____

_____

_____

_____

OCTOBER 12

I'm most myself when I _____.

Year: _____

_____

_____

_____

_____

Year: _____

_____

_____

_____

_____

Year: _____

_____

_____

_____

_____

OCTOBER 13

Who would you love to get a call from?

Year: _____

_____

_____

_____

_____

Year: _____

_____

_____

_____

_____

Year: _____

_____

_____

_____

_____

OCTOBER 14

When have you been stronger
than you knew?

Year: _____

_____

_____

_____

_____

Year: _____

_____

_____

_____

_____

Year: _____

_____

_____

_____

_____

OCTOBER 15

Let go of something that's been bothering
you by writing it down.

Year: _____

_____
_____
_____
_____

Year: _____

_____
_____
_____
_____

Year: _____

_____
_____
_____
_____

OCTOBER 16

Today is going to be _____.

Year: _____

_____

_____

_____

_____

Year: _____

_____

_____

_____

_____

Year: _____

_____

_____

_____

_____

OCTOBER 17

Something joyful I can add to my life is _____.

Year: _____

_____

_____

_____

_____

Year: _____

_____

_____

_____

_____

Year: _____

_____

_____

_____

_____

OCTOBER 18

What is your favorite flower?

Year: _____

_____
_____
_____
_____

Year: _____

_____
_____
_____
_____

Year: _____

_____
_____
_____
_____

OCTOBER 19

I will stop giving myself a hard time
about _____.

Year: _____

_____

_____

_____

_____

Year: _____

_____

_____

_____

_____

Year: _____

_____

_____

_____

_____

OCTOBER 20

Book a table at your favorite restaurant.
What will you order?

Year: _____

_____

_____

_____

_____

Year: _____

_____

_____

_____

_____

Year: _____

_____

_____

_____

_____

OCTOBER 21

Make a lunch date with your favorite
person. Who will it be?

Year: _____

_____

_____

_____

_____

Year: _____

_____

_____

_____

_____

Year: _____

_____

_____

_____

_____

OCTOBER 22

Add a fun detour to your commute today.
Where will you go?

Year: _____

_____

_____

_____

_____

Year: _____

_____

_____

_____

_____

Year: _____

_____

_____

_____

_____

OCTOBER 23

Update your profile pic. What's one thing you
love about the new photo?

Year: _____

_____

_____

_____

_____

Year: _____

_____

_____

_____

_____

Year: _____

_____

_____

_____

_____

OCTOBER 24

Change your ringtone to something that makes you smile. What song or sound will it be?

Year: _____

_____

_____

_____

Year: _____

_____

_____

_____

Year: _____

_____

_____

_____

OCTOBER 25

Why do you deserve a raise or a promotion?

Year: _____

_____

_____

_____

_____

Year: _____

_____

_____

_____

_____

Year: _____

_____

_____

_____

_____

OCTOBER 26

Someday I will achieve _____.

Year: _____

_____

_____

_____

_____

Year: _____

_____

_____

_____

_____

Year: _____

_____

_____

_____

_____

OCTOBER 27

What makes you unstoppable?

Year: _____

_____

_____

_____

_____

Year: _____

_____

_____

_____

_____

Year: _____

_____

_____

_____

_____

OCTOBER 28

What makes you loveable?

Year: _____

_____

_____

_____

_____

Year: _____

_____

_____

_____

_____

Year: _____

_____

_____

_____

_____

OCTOBER 29

What will you invite into your life this week?

Year: _____

_____

_____

_____

_____

Year: _____

_____

_____

_____

_____

Year: _____

_____

_____

_____

_____

OCTOBER 30

What makes you a catch?

Year: _____

_____

_____

_____

_____

Year: _____

_____

_____

_____

_____

Year: _____

_____

_____

_____

_____

OCTOBER 31

What fear have you overcome?

Year: _____

_____

_____

_____

_____

Year: _____

_____

_____

_____

_____

Year: _____

_____

_____

_____

_____

NOVEMBER 1

What are you looking forward
to doing this month?

Year: _____

_____

_____

_____

_____

Year: _____

_____

_____

_____

_____

Year: _____

_____

_____

_____

_____

NOVEMBER 2

This year I will _____.

Year: _____

_____
_____
_____
_____

Year: _____

_____
_____
_____
_____

Year: _____

_____
_____
_____
_____

NOVEMBER 3

Write down three small changes that
could bring extra joy.

Year: _____

_____
_____
_____
_____

Year: _____

_____
_____
_____
_____

Year: _____

_____
_____
_____
_____

NOVEMBER 4

After a long day, there's nothing better
than a _____.

Year: _____

_____

_____

_____

_____

Year: _____

_____

_____

_____

_____

Year: _____

_____

_____

_____

_____

NOVEMBER 5

When I'm feeling confident,
I can _____.

Year: _____

_____

_____

_____

_____

Year: _____

_____

_____

_____

_____

Year: _____

_____

_____

_____

_____

NOVEMBER 6

In what areas of your life have you
found the most success?

Year: _____

_____

_____

_____

_____

Year: _____

_____

_____

_____

_____

Year: _____

_____

_____

_____

_____

NOVEMBER 7

Whose expectations have you surpassed?

Year: _____

_____

_____

_____

_____

Year: _____

_____

_____

_____

_____

Year: _____

_____

_____

_____

_____

NOVEMBER 8

How can you spread goodwill today?

Year: _____

_____
_____
_____
_____

Year: _____

_____
_____
_____
_____

Year: _____

_____
_____
_____
_____

NOVEMBER 9

Who needs you (in a good way)?

Year: _____

_____

_____

_____

_____

Year: _____

_____

_____

_____

_____

Year: _____

_____

_____

_____

_____

NOVEMBER 10

What are you idealistic about?

Year: _____

_____

_____

_____

_____

Year: _____

_____

_____

_____

_____

Year: _____

_____

_____

_____

_____

NOVEMBER 11

What is the most satisfying part of your day?

Year: _____

_____

_____

_____

_____

Year: _____

_____

_____

_____

_____

Year: _____

_____

_____

_____

_____

NOVEMBER 12

How are you still evolving?

Year: _____

_____

_____

_____

_____

Year: _____

_____

_____

_____

_____

Year: _____

_____

_____

_____

_____

NOVEMBER 13

When have you needed a fresh start?
What would that look like now?

Year: _____

_____

_____

_____

_____

Year: _____

_____

_____

_____

_____

Year: _____

_____

_____

_____

_____

NOVEMBER 14

What could you watch
all day long?

Year: _____

_____

_____

_____

_____

Year: _____

_____

_____

_____

_____

Year: _____

_____

_____

_____

_____

NOVEMBER 15

Which friendship or relationship is blooming?

Year: _____

_____

_____

_____

_____

Year: _____

_____

_____

_____

_____

Year: _____

_____

_____

_____

_____

NOVEMBER 16

I am hopeful that _____.

Year: _____

_____

_____

_____

_____

Year: _____

_____

_____

_____

_____

Year: _____

_____

_____

_____

_____

NOVEMBER 17

Sometimes it's the little things that bring the
greatest joy. What are those things in your life?

Year: _____

_____

_____

_____

_____

Year: _____

_____

_____

_____

_____

Year: _____

_____

_____

_____

_____

NOVEMBER 18

I will measure this day by _____.

Year: _____

_____

_____

_____

_____

Year: _____

_____

_____

_____

_____

Year: _____

_____

_____

_____

_____

NOVEMBER 19

Something brave I can do is _____.

Year: _____

_____

_____

_____

_____

Year: _____

_____

_____

_____

_____

Year: _____

_____

_____

_____

_____

NOVEMBER 20

What opportunities are you ready to take?

Year: _____

_____

_____

_____

_____

Year: _____

_____

_____

_____

_____

Year: _____

_____

_____

_____

_____

NOVEMBER 21

How will you seize this day?

Year: _____

_____
_____
_____
_____

Year: _____

_____
_____
_____
_____

Year: _____

_____
_____
_____
_____

NOVEMBER 22

What neighborly thing could you do today?

Year: _____

_____
_____
_____
_____

Year: _____

_____
_____
_____
_____

Year: _____

_____
_____
_____
_____

NOVEMBER 23

Make a bold promise to yourself or
someone you love.

Year: _____

_____

_____

_____

_____

Year: _____

_____

_____

_____

_____

Year: _____

_____

_____

_____

_____

NOVEMBER 24

Make a bright prediction
about your future.

Year: _____

_____

_____

_____

_____

Year: _____

_____

_____

_____

_____

Year: _____

_____

_____

_____

_____

NOVEMBER 25

Look for the best in someone today.
What do you see?

Year: _____

_____

_____

_____

_____

Year: _____

_____

_____

_____

_____

Year: _____

_____

_____

_____

_____

NOVEMBER 26

Every day is a chance to _____.

Year: _____

_____
_____
_____
_____

Year: _____

_____
_____
_____
_____

Year: _____

_____
_____
_____
_____

NOVEMBER 27

What do you appreciate about
your hometown?

Year: _____

_____

_____

_____

_____

Year: _____

_____

_____

_____

_____

Year: _____

_____

_____

_____

_____

NOVEMBER 28

Who or what gets an A+
from you today?

Year: _____

_____

_____

_____

_____

Year: _____

_____

_____

_____

_____

Year: _____

_____

_____

_____

_____

NOVEMBER 29

What values keep you steady
and grounded?

Year: _____

_____

_____

_____

_____

Year: _____

_____

_____

_____

_____

Year: _____

_____

_____

_____

_____

NOVEMBER 30

What could you look at from
a different angle?

Year: _____

_____

_____

_____

_____

Year: _____

_____

_____

_____

_____

Year: _____

_____

_____

_____

_____

DECEMBER 1

Which shows and movies
encourage positivity?

Year: _____

_____

_____

_____

_____

Year: _____

_____

_____

_____

_____

Year: _____

_____

_____

_____

_____

DECEMBER 2

Snap a photo of something joyful
today, then describe it.

Year: _____

_____

_____

_____

_____

Year: _____

_____

_____

_____

_____

Year: _____

_____

_____

_____

_____

DECEMBER 3

Describe something positive you found on social
media today. Share it with others.

Year: _____

_____

_____

_____

_____

Year: _____

_____

_____

_____

_____

Year: _____

_____

_____

_____

_____

DECEMBER 4

When has the truth set you free?

Year: _____

_____
_____
_____
_____

Year: _____

_____
_____
_____
_____

Year: _____

_____
_____
_____
_____

DECEMBER 5

I look forward to the day I _____.

Year: _____

_____

_____

_____

_____

Year: _____

_____

_____

_____

_____

Year: _____

_____

_____

_____

_____

DECEMBER 6

Who lets you vent?

Year: _____

_____

_____

_____

_____

Year: _____

_____

_____

_____

_____

Year: _____

_____

_____

_____

_____

DECEMBER 7

Who helps you shine?

Year: _____

_____

_____

_____

_____

Year: _____

_____

_____

_____

_____

Year: _____

_____

_____

_____

_____

DECEMBER 8

What's a sign of progress in the world?

Year: _____

_____

_____

_____

_____

Year: _____

_____

_____

_____

_____

Year: _____

_____

_____

_____

_____

DECEMBER 9

What's a sign of progress in your life?

Year: _____

_____

_____

_____

_____

Year: _____

_____

_____

_____

_____

Year: _____

_____

_____

_____

_____

DECEMBER 10

What makes your heart pound?

Year: _____

_____

_____

_____

_____

Year: _____

_____

_____

_____

_____

Year: _____

_____

_____

_____

_____

DECEMBER 11

What do you hope to discover?

Year: _____

_____

_____

_____

_____

Year: _____

_____

_____

_____

_____

Year: _____

_____

_____

_____

_____

DECEMBER 12

My goal for today is _____.

Year: _____

_____

_____

_____

_____

Year: _____

_____

_____

_____

_____

Year: _____

_____

_____

_____

_____

DECEMBER 13

What past mistake can you laugh about now?

Year: _____

_____

_____

_____

_____

Year: _____

_____

_____

_____

_____

Year: _____

_____

_____

_____

_____

DECEMBER 14

What small victory can you celebrate?

Year: _____

_____

_____

_____

_____

Year: _____

_____

_____

_____

_____

Year: _____

_____

_____

_____

_____

DECEMBER 15

Who understands you?

Year: _____

_____
_____
_____
_____

Year: _____

_____
_____
_____
_____

Year: _____

_____
_____
_____
_____

DECEMBER 16

Watch the sunrise or sunset today
and describe its beauty.

Year: _____

_____

_____

_____

_____

Year: _____

_____

_____

_____

_____

Year: _____

_____

_____

_____

_____

DECEMBER 17

When have you turned something ordinary
into something extraordinary?

Year: _____

_____

_____

_____

_____

Year: _____

_____

_____

_____

_____

Year: _____

_____

_____

_____

_____

DECEMBER 18

What reflects your unique spirit?

Year: _____

_____
_____
_____
_____

Year: _____

_____
_____
_____
_____

Year: _____

_____
_____
_____
_____

DECEMBER 19

If you could be reincarnated, who or
what would you want to be?

Year: _____

_____
_____
_____
_____

Year: _____

_____
_____
_____
_____

Year: _____

_____
_____
_____
_____

DECEMBER 20

When you imagine your future, what do
you care about most?

Year: _____

_____

_____

_____

_____

Year: _____

_____

_____

_____

_____

Year: _____

_____

_____

_____

_____

DECEMBER 21

What wisdom would you give
your younger self?

Year: _____

_____

_____

_____

_____

Year: _____

_____

_____

_____

_____

Year: _____

_____

_____

_____

_____

DECEMBER 22

Who or what brightens your day?

Year: _____

_____

_____

_____

_____

Year: _____

_____

_____

_____

_____

Year: _____

_____

_____

_____

_____

DECEMBER 23

What rule do you want to live by?

Year: _____

_____

_____

_____

_____

Year: _____

_____

_____

_____

_____

Year: _____

_____

_____

_____

_____

DECEMBER 24

What would you like to dream about tonight?

Year: _____

_____

_____

_____

_____

Year: _____

_____

_____

_____

_____

Year: _____

_____

_____

_____

_____

DECEMBER 25

I believe in _____.

Year: _____

_____

_____

_____

_____

Year: _____

_____

_____

_____

_____

Year: _____

_____

_____

_____

_____

DECEMBER 26

I draw my strength from _____.

Year: _____

_____

_____

_____

_____

Year: _____

_____

_____

_____

_____

Year: _____

_____

_____

_____

_____

DECEMBER 27

What never ceases to amaze you?

Year: _____

_____
_____
_____
_____

Year: _____

_____
_____
_____
_____

Year: _____

_____
_____
_____
_____

DECEMBER 28

What doors have been opened for you?

Year: _____

_____

_____

_____

_____

Year: _____

_____

_____

_____

_____

Year: _____

_____

_____

_____

_____

DECEMBER 29

What are you doing right?

Year: _____

_____

_____

_____

_____

Year: _____

_____

_____

_____

_____

Year: _____

_____

_____

_____

_____

DECEMBER 30

How can you let more sunshine into your life,
literally or figuratively?

Year: _____

_____

_____

_____

_____

Year: _____

_____

_____

_____

_____

Year: _____

_____

_____

_____

_____

DECEMBER 31

Today is the perfect day to _____.

Year: _____

_____

_____

_____

_____

Year: _____

_____

_____

_____

_____

Year: _____

_____

_____

_____

_____